Knowledge Books and Software

Western Australia has many special places. One of these is the islands off the Kimberleys. These are called the Buccaneer Islands. This area is home to the Mayala people.

Knowledge Books and Software

3

A long time ago, the sea was a lot lower. The First Peoples could walk a long way towards Indonesia. Australia was joined to Papua New Guinea. This time was called the Ice Age.

Knowledge Books and Software

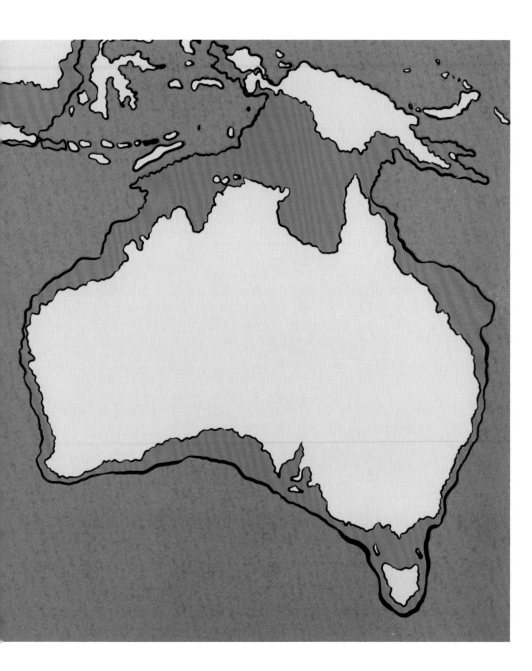

5

The First Peoples saw many big animals. One looked like a giant wombat. There were giant birds much bigger than emus. Some lizards were as big as crocodiles!

7

The Ice Age ended about 10,000 years ago. The sea level rose over 100 metres. Many places were now underwater. Islands formed when the water flooded the lands.

Knowledge Books and Software

9

The Mayala people still visited the islands. The people fished and hunted in the waters. They built stone shelters to help stop the strong winds.

Knowledge Books and Software

11

The Mayala people are still in this area. They have not lived on the islands for a long time. They come and go. There is very little fresh water on the islands. People have been living in this area for over 50,000 years.

13

Before the sea level rose, the climate was different. The people hunted over this area. Stone tools have been found on the seafloor close to these islands.

Knowledge Books and Software

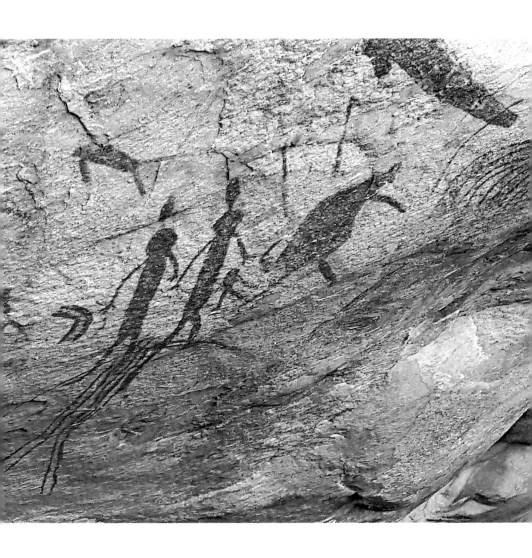

15

People from Asia and Europe sailed here. This was a long time before the First Fleet. The Macassans and the pearlers stayed in this area. The Dutch and the Portuguese sailed into this area. The First Nations people made drawings of them.

The Mayala people have been here for many thousands of years. The islands were named after a buccaneer called William Dampier. Dampier made maps of this area.

19

Tides are huge in the Buccaneer Islands. The sea level can change by up to 12 metres in just 12 hours. This can cause the water to rush quickly off the reefs at low tide. Montgomery Reef has waterfalls from the tides.

Knowledge Books and Software

Knowledge Books and Software

Iron ore has been mined on Cockatoo and Kulan Islands. The ore is loaded straight onto ships. The other islands are popular for fishing and tourism. First Nations people take good care of the Buccaneer Islands. They are a very important part of their history and culture.

Knowledge Books and Software

Word bank

Cockatoo	Kimberleys
Koolan	Western Australia
Montgomery	drawings
Buccaneers	tides
Dampier	levels
waterfalls	climate
Dutch	different
Portuguese	shelters
islands	Indonesia
Mayala	tourism
explorers	important
pearlers	culture
Macassans	

Knowledge Books and Software